# BEHIND THE BRICKS III
## WRITING AND ART FROM
## THE CROW WING COUNTY JAIL
## 2013-2014

PUBLISHED BY:

RIVER
PLACE
PRESS

201 West Laurel Street
Brainerd, MN 56401
www.riverplacepress.com
218.851.4843

ISBN: 978-0-9903563-1-8
Copyright RiverPlace Press, 2014

Designed and Produced by Chip and Jean Borkenhagen

Representation and Promotion by Blue Cottage Agency
www.bluecottageagency.com

Printed in the United States at Bang Printing, Brainerd, MN.

# CONTENTS

The one thing that you have that nobody else has is you.
Your voice, your mind, your story, your vision.
So write and draw and build and play and dance and
live as only you can.

*~ Neil Gaiman*

# INTRODUCTION

Being incarcerated can be difficult. Understandably, for many, it is a time of self-examination and figuring out how to live in ways that won't bring them back to jail. Inmates are asking important questions about who they are and who they want to be. We believe that the arts can play a part in helping people deal with those questions.

The literacy program at the Crow Wing County Jail began several years ago with Fathers Reading Every Day (FRED). FRED is a national program aimed at increasing children's success in school by promoting early literacy experiences in families. Back then FRED leader Lowell Johnson envisioned broadening the program, and in four years it has expanded to book clubs, writing groups and visual art classes led by instructors who guide the inmates in productive self-expression.

This year a grant from the Five Wings Arts Council, with matching funds from the Crossing Arts Alliance, has enabled the project to expand its programs, publish a third book and produce a new and exciting arts and writing exhibit. In an effort to connect inmates to the wider artistic community, artists and writers on the outside selected inmate work and created companion pieces to complement the originals. Exhibits at the Crow Wing County Jail and at the Q Gallery in the Franklin Arts Center included both the original work and companion pieces.

The volunteers are the heart and soul of the programs. In addition to their artistic and literary expertise, they bring kindness, respect, empathy and laughter to everything they do. Huge thank-yous to Doris Anderson, Lily Atwel, Sandy Bergstrom, Tammy Dewey, Char Donovan, Sara Egan, Elsie Husom, Lowell Johnson, Lonnie Knutson, Shari Krizek, Karen Lundblad, Marcia Mans, Sandy Nielsen, Nancy Palmer, Connie O'Brien, Karen Ogdahl, Maurice Olson, Margaret Steblay and Maria Thompson-Seep.

In addition to the support of the Five Wings Arts Council, we would like to thank these other generous donors: Anderson Family Foundation, Brainerd Area Retired Educators, Gesner Johnson Family Foundation, The Mille Lacs Band of Ojibwe, Monday Afternoon Book Group at Lord of Life Lutheran Church, Presbytery of MN Valleys and Wednesday Morning Club of The Center.

Many thanks to Ron Morris of Brainerd InstyPrints, Chip and Jean Borkenhagen of RiverPlace Press, Joey Halvorson, Dave Boran and Lisa Jordan for their assistance with the book's production. Special thanks to Project Leaders Krista Rolfzen Soukup and Elsie Husom and Instruction Leader Karen Ogdahl for their expertise and creativity in the conception and implementation of this project.

Also, thanks go to Sheriff Todd Dahl, the Crow Wing County Jail administration, Programs Sergeant Miranda Neuwirth and staff for their welcoming and cheerful cooperation with scheduling, storage of supplies, admitting volunteers through the many doors each visit and assistance in details of the project.

Above all, gratitude must go to the program participants, the inmates, who are willing to share their viewpoints, talents and dreams with the wider community. Here are a few of their comments about the literacy program:

"It's very important to feel like you belong to something when you are in a situation like this."

"It was great allowing us to create from our hearts."

"I have gained ways of expressing my feelings in a non-hostile atmosphere and ways to improve my writing and realizing that it can be accepted and helpful to others."

Those of us who volunteer at the jail feel that our artistic and literary programs are more than just ways to help pass the time. We believe they can be valuable components in the rehabilitation process, and we are so grateful to be part of that process. We hope you enjoy this sampling of the writing and art that was produced Behind the Bricks.

*For more information about the jail programs or if you are interested in volunteering, contact Programs Sergeant Miranda Neuwirth at 218-822-7067 or miranda.neuwirth@crowwing.us.*

These activities are funded, in part, by the Minnesota arts and heritage fund as appropriated by the Minnesota State Legislature with money from the vote of the people of Minnesota on November 4, 2008.

## The Pause Factor

*Joseph Clark*

Jail has a way of changing a person. It's not so much being in jail that causes the change; it's the pause factor. See, life outside of jail doesn't stop; it doesn't even slow down. But in jail it does. It's like your life got put on pause and you have no control of the remote. Your life comes to a grinding halt while the rest of the world moves on.

You count days, hoping they go by fast, while the rest of the world is amazed by how time flies. Each day inside is another day you can never get back, and almost no one even notices you're gone. Your kids and girlfriend learn how to live without you; your family moves on; your friends find new friends.

You spend all of your days thinking about what you should have done and what you're gonna do. When you've thought so much that you've finally decided that you are the root of all evil and that by changing how you act, the rest of the world will change too, then you are just getting started.

Those who are lucky have an out date, and the rest wait in limbo. But, eventually your day comes and you get out only to find that you have nothing left. Everything you thought about doesn't matter because while you sat and thought, the rest of the world moved on, and you're left trying to put the broken pieces back together.

But, you have no glue. So, what do you do?

Give up!

## The Grandmas and Grandpas

*Dennis Brown*

The things the grandmas and grandpas sacrificed so we could hold on to our traditions. The ceremony, the language, our sacred items, the story, the songs, the dances, all our traditions, our heritage to pass down to the children and our children's children. Things that have been hidden away, practiced secretly for fear of being beaten, jailed, killed. Punished for being the way their grandpas and grandmas have passed down to them for being Native American.

The sweat lodge – they would meet deep in the woods each bringing blankets, sacred medicines, sacred items, pipes, rattles, drums and feathers. They gathered the right kind of wood and rocks. Iron wood for the ribs, jack pine for the fire. They put everything together, had a ceremony, a small feast thanking the spirits for being with them.

When you were small, did you ever wonder why the grandmas and grandpas used to stop speaking the language when someone walked in the room and switch to English without missing a beat or syllable? Gramps told me his mouth was washed out with lye soap or he was locked in the basement cubbyhole of the school. Hair pulled, slapped, beaten with a belt or switch so they would meet in private to sneak speaking the language. They didn't know it but they were saving it for their children.

The songs and dances – you call them powwows but to us they are celebrations. Some are ceremonies like the Jingle Dress Dance. This is a sacred dance. Its origin came about when a boy was hurt real bad and was in the hospital. His mother was there all the time praying and talking to the boy who was in a coma. She wasn't eating or sleeping. After four days she had a vision. The spirits told her to make a dress. Some say the first one was made with tobacco ties all over the dress. After that the tobacco ties were replaced by jingles made of snuff container tops. In this vision, she was also given a song and a special dance to do in a ceremony. As she was coming to the end of the dance, the young man woke up and made a full recovery.

Many stories and legends were passed down. The grandpas and grandmas sacrificed so much so we could hold on to who we are as people. Be proud to be Anish-a-naba, the first people. Respect your elders and care for them. The things they know is who we are.

This is the way I heard it. You may hear these stories in a somewhat different way.

## Cayla

*Sonya Garbow*

Feeling down, depressed, sad and alone,
empty of all but a suicidal thought.
Thinking of how my daughter feels
and the mother she thinks I'm not.
I know I'm not the best,
I know I've even done some wrong.
I've tried to make this right,
but this road I'm walking seems so long.
I know I asked for forgiveness.
I know I've even screamed, "Please!"
I know I said I love you,
even got down on my knees.
I asked the Lord, if I can,
to see your beautiful smile,
and a picture of you pops in my head
I haven't seen in a while.
I know I can't take away the pain
of how you feel inside.
Just know deep in my heart, my daughter,
your love will always reside.
Even tho' I wronged you,
even tho' I left you alone.
All this time, in my mind,
your beauty's always shown.
You're the diamonds in my eyes,
the gold around my heart.
Tho' millions of miles between us, my girl,
we'll never be apart.
Know that I love you,
I'll even walk through the gates of hell
to say that I need you,
for even God himself can't tell.
My love for you will shine
like royalty to make your life anew.
So smile for me, my girl,
'cuz mommy's always loving you.

**Away**

*Keri Zelinske*

I close my eyes
and there you are.
But when they open, you're gone -
my shooting stars.
I miss your giggles,
I miss your hugs;
I miss your screams
whenever there's a bug.
It breaks my heart
and shakes my soul,
because you need me –
this I know.
We'll be together again
some day soon,
but for now, remember,
I love you to the moon!

## Dead Inside

*Kirk Nelson*

You've killed all my feelings.
I don't care no more;
I just keep self-destructing.
My life can't be easy
because you see to that.
You seek to keep my heart broken;
you make my loved ones lie to me.
You make them steal my stuff
and stomp on my heart.
You're a fake and I see it now.
Just too bad I had to lose it all
before I opened my eyes.
You're evil and you steal people's lives.
You're a sick bastard
and I rebuke you.
Go away!
God is now taking over.
so really, in the end, who's the real fool?
You are, Sucker!

**Behind My Paint**

*Nathan Schnaufer*

To show what's behind my paint, my mask, my façade of life is to let people see who truly lies within my head. Do I even know enough to show what lies within, or am I just as lost as the ones closest? Striving, digging, begging for an answer or even an inkling as to what's behind the paint.

I sit here day after day with the face paint on - a hardened, seasoned Juggalo. My expression never changing much, the thoughts mixed up behind the paint never showing much emotion, never wanting to show much emotion.

To show emotion shows weakness; or does it? Is that the reason for the paint?

My loved ones all see me as pushing away, closing off; but I can feel myself screaming out, wanting, needing – my voice always seems to fall short. My emotion, my feelings only expressed by the painted smile of the stern, straight business-like look of the clown at the surface.

"Conditioned by the past," is what some people say. "Born without emotions," say others. "Masked by the paint," is what I say!

Is it possible in my mind for the feelings inside and the paint on the surface to co-exist? There's gotta be a middle ground, a place for them both to ride what I call the merry-go-round. A place in what everyone calls Life.

## Let Go

*Amelia Frazer*

Let go of all the bad,
releasing it like I never have.
      I no longer want to be locked-down.

Take this frown, turn it around,
I want a real smile
      to stay more than awhile.

Just to let go of it all,
Even if I may stumble and fall
      I know I will always get back up.

It's like a volcano ready to erupt.
I am ready to release it all
      Never again to be stuck between the walls.

I'm slowly letting go of all the hurt
knowing I still need to put in a lot of work.
"I can do it," I tell myself, hoping to really believe
      that I will succeed and find relief
      from what got me to this point in life.

I'm done with all this turmoil and strife.
I can let it go without feeling bad,
looking forward to all I've never had –
      real happiness and joy surrounding my soul,
      never to be drug down again to this black hole.

## Opened Eyes

*Daniel C. May*

As I continue this battle, I soon began to realize. It took me awhile too, but once I did, something began to rise! I thought my soul was gone, but it was in hiding this whole entire time. Being in here has done nothing more than open my eyes, because I had forgotten what being clean and sober felt like.

## How Will I Laugh Tomorrow When I Can't Even Smile Today?

*Jeffrey*

Here I sit and watch my world come crumbling down.
I cry for help but no one is around.
Silently screaming as I bang my head against the wall,
it seems like no one, no one cares at all.
There's always an emotion, but how can I explain?
It's like a scent of a rose with words I can't express - my pain.
I'm caught up in emotion going over my head;
some times, I think to myself, "Am I living or dead?"

The clock keeps ticking but nothing seems to change;
my problems are never solved, they're just rearranged.
Then I think about the times I had –
Some are good, but most are bad.
I search for personality and those things inside of me,
Peace and love flash through my mind,
but pain and hate is all I ever find.
I found no hope in nothing new,
and I never had a dream come true.

If I'm going to die, Lord, take away my fears.
If I'm going to cry, Lord, wipe away my tears.
But before I drown in sorrow, I just want to say,
"How will I laugh tomorrow when I can't even smile today?

Signed: Lonely and Caged

## You Could Be Anywhere

*Celeste Nelson-Raba*

My mom says being in jail is like being nowhere, so why not be any-where?

On Monday, she says she loves me and how is sunny California?

On Tuesday, she says be positive, she loves me, and how is the weather in Dallas?

On Wednesday, she says I love you! It's cold here; how is Arizona?

On Thursday, she says I miss you. How is Mexico?

On Friday, she says I hope you're winning big in Vegas. The family wishes you luck.

On Saturday, she says I hope you didn't get burnt in South America. I wish I could be there with you.

On Sunday, she says I love you and I miss you, and no matter where you are, you're always in my heart and on my mind.

## My Mom Says

*Celeste Nelson-Raba*

My mom says...
        This is where it starts;
        whether it's prison or treatment or freedom you seek,
            this is where it starts.
        Whether it's God or sobriety or just a chance to slow down,
            this is where it starts.

My mom says...
        Take a deep breath
        Look inside yourself
        Weigh and measure every decision
        Be thorough and confident
        Keep your head up
        Be positive and remember
            your mom says ...

This is where your new life starts!

## Welcome

*Stephanie Johnson*

Silly is a blessing
brought to me
Unexpected in this place
under lock and key.

Who are we?
Women of varied traits.
Where are we?
Jail – what happened to my date?

Last things remembered
before placed here
like dinner and dancing
maybe a few beers.

Or a joyride with friends
innocently unaware
others' personal affairs
become yours to bear.

Fear is among us
feeling so weak.
Time seems endless and
our brains start to freak.

"Hello, my name is..."
And so it begins
Strangers become friends
despite our sins.

Silly is a blessing
I bring to you
"Hello, my name is....
How are you?

## A Talk with Self

*James Richmond*

"You ought to be ashamed of yourself
          for having these selfish ways,
Never taking into consideration
          how you may affect someone else's day.

Every impulsive decision you make
          leads down a road of strife;
I wonder does it have an effect
          on how you may ruin your loved one's life?

I have to close my eyes
          cause I can't bear to watch you go down the drain.
You're the reason St. Peter's got started
          for the mentally insane.

It's funny how you get in trouble
          and a whole other person enters your mind.
You're the only person I know
          who doesn't have a problem walking blind.

What do you tell your kids when they
          want you to take them to the park and play?
You probably got "tomorrow" on repeat
          and it never becomes today.

Do you have a significant other
          who's always complaining about your attention?
Love is just a word in the dictionary
          that's hard to verbally mention."

I open my eyes and retain my focus
          unable to maintain my concentration
Then look at him looking at me looking at him;
          I'm done with this conversation!

### 3 Tier

*Josephine Andrews*

Six by eight.
That's all the space
for twenty-one hours I'll have to face.
Five hundred and sixty blocks.
Left alone with all my thoughts.
Thinking of ways to escape
Knowing damn well that's not my fate
I won't come back; you know it's true
because six by eight is too small a room.

## Invisible Mail

*Larry Olson*

The strangest thing happened today,
The invisible mailman passed my way.
He handed me something that wasn't really there
And said "To receive invisible mail is really rare."
So I opened this nothing, opened it wide
And found the unexpected, nothing inside.
The scent was sweet as I recall,
So sweet, in fact, there was no scent at all.
The penmanship was neat and clean,
So neat, in fact, it couldn't be seen.
So now I write to you, the self-proclaimed good friend
Because you said you'd be there 'til the very end.
Now I think of you and question your meaning of a friend.
I wait and wait for the letter you always said you'd send.
I could be out there soon and making life much better,
And you could be in here waiting for a letter.

## She Talks to Angels

*Anna Anderson*

I feel you everywhere I go, like angels that stand two feet high, clinging to my ankles – a longing I never knew I could feel. It's metaphoric of the child I never had.

Tears flow and plant roots under my toes as I dig my feet deep in the soil, and it allows me to repatch our mismatched patchwork quilt again.

You are still a part of my family tree, Baby I never had. You just seem to linger amongst the leaves. In my hair, you're the breeze; you're the star beyond the trees that will forever reflect in my eye and cast your shadow on my heart.

I now call my scars my stars, for you will always be with me. Maybe not as my right hand, but more like night and day.

I did it for a reason...it made the woman I am today.

## A Friend Just Like You

*Marissa Lueck*

Are we friends, or are we not?
You told me once, but I forgot.
So tell me now and tell me true,
So I can say, "I'm here for you."
Of all the friends I've ever met,
You're the one I won't forget.
And if I die before you do,
I'll go to Heaven and wait for you.
I'll give the angels back their wings
And risk the loss of everything!
There isn't a thing I wouldn't do
To have a friend just like you.

## Lost and Found

*Anthoni McMorris-Rice*

He lost his happiness when he lost his mother. From that horrifying day when she lay still, body as limp as a paralyzed leg, without a pint of air to fill her lungs, his soul became dark. His world became corrupted. A black veil descended over his eyes, and no one ever saw joy in his face again. His heart, that once was full of generosity, kindness and love, became drained and refilled with murder, deceit and hate.

He roamed the streets like a mad animal, preying upon the weak. Took hostage the innocence of those who cared for him. Chopped off the hands of those who tried reaching out to him. Stuffed, with cloth drenched in gasoline, the mouths of those who spoke nothing but kind words to him, for he was afraid that those kind words would do nothing but burn his soul - reigniting those haunting memories that had turned his spirit into ashes long ago. The flames in his eyes danced like demons in Hades when a new member comes among them. His blood boiled to the point in which it was mistaken for magma. His ire was that of a raging bull with red painted all around it. He spared no one.

No one was safe from this beast you called a child. No one but I. I was he. I was that beast you called a child.

But that beast died at the hands of a warrior who feared nothing. A warrior whose armor was as shiny as a polished gold nugget. A warrior who covered flaws with his long leather cape and drank gasoline to fuel his ambition and dedication to destroy such a beast. A warrior far greater than those from Greece.

I am forever grateful that I'd found this warrior who, then and now, resides in me.

## Parade

*Annie Kinzer*

Who knew
We'd all look so great in blue?
The guys all stare as they wait.
They probably wonder, could it be fate?
As we march by like a small parade,
One of us might be wearing a braid.
We follow like sheep
But don't dare make a peep
Or hum a hymn
On our way to the gym.

## Odd Collection

*Hunter Vidnar*

I've got an odd collection – I call them scars.
They each have a story and a past.
Some are part of me; some you cannot see.
Some I put there to feel the pain.
Some are deep or thin; others round
      like one on my knee when I fell on the ground.

Too many to count; too much hurt to remember.
One of my worst I got in December.
It's on my left wrist cause I thought
      it would be bliss to be rid of the pain.
Now it's my prize possession in my odd collection.
It's a reminder of who I once was.

      We all got scars – maps of our past,
      but, just know, the pain doesn't last.

## Not Guilty

*Shenowa*

My mouth is dry; my vision is blurred.
My breath smells like liquor; my speech is slurred.
There's blood on my hands;
There's blood on my face;
There's blood on my clothes;
I just caught a case.
There are police all around
screaming, "Get to the ground!"

She's a villain turned victim.
That's how the story goes,
but it's more than it seems
and the evidence shows.
A riot? An assault? I say, "Self-defense."
What was said in the statements –
it just doesn't make sense.

I sit and I wait, I wait and I sit,
Waiting for trial on a crime I didn't commit.
They'll offer a plea, I'm not taking it, Nope!
I stand only with pride, holding on to hope.
Days turn to weeks, turn to months.
Suddenly everything hits me at once.
The train to freedom comes to a halt;
I hope they see the truth, I'm not at fault.
Not Guilty....

**Stuff**

*Name Withheld*

I remember it like it was yesterday. It's burned into my memories, a rite of passage, a hallmark in time, like a bad burn.

Hot out that night, full moon, no bugs out and there was a scent of gas and tar paper in the air. A song called "Baker Street" was on a radio somewhere, lots of houses on tract then – new people, all Indians but city Indians.

They said I was square; even country Skins said I was square; didn't matter to me though.

It was real peaceful until the moment I knew that I had crossed the line. Life would never be the same again!

I was in a jail cell getting really psyched up for battle. If this went down the right way, somebody would die; it didn't matter to me either way.

Then all of a sudden, I realized the light in the cell wasn't coming from the light bulb; it was right in front of me, and it was amber mellow light. It was a presence! I didn't actually see it like words or hear it like a voice or sense it like a really good idea. But it was like all three happening at once.

It said, "You will never be alone again," and I felt like I had stepped into a warm shower or rain storm. The feeling that came over me was peace, even though I didn't know it at the time.

## You Only Need to Know
A piece for my 5-year-old son, Marik Michael Malaki

*Tonya Marie Stalwick*

If you ask me, I miss you;
tears stream down my face.
I can't put in words how much I love you.
I'd give you the sun, the world and stars in space.
You are my light, my life,
My son, my mini me.
As you watch the world around you –
the hustle, the bustle, the people passing by,
your beautiful face filled with wonder, the image in your eyes
bluer than the sky.
I'll do anything to protect you, always hold you dear;
I won't shelter you from life
for it will only cause more fear.
I'll take you anywhere you want to go.
higher than the mountains
or in the rugged valleys below,
hold you when you're sleepy til you finally close your eyes.
I pray you have sweet, peaceful dreams
until again the sun shall rise.
There will be lessons you learn in this life;
there'll be happiness, sadness,
great triumph and great strife.
I hope you look above you
for answers near and far.
I pray you never give up faith
and make a wish in every passing star.
I cannot lay a path to follow
nor can I rush to you at every stumble,
though hard your falls, I must allow,
but I'll always be there standing proud
and help you dust yourself back off.
Your strength will come from all the struggles
you endure on this earthly place.

Always remember, your sins are forgotten
and you shall never fall from grace.
So, my dear son, know I love you forever and ever
until our forever is never; then our eternal love will start.
You started in my belly, my love,
but you'll forever live in my heart.

## My Angela

*Jane Parker*

Long brown hair – big bright eyes
Invisible wings like butterflies
The path for her – long and straight
Her future filled – with beauteous fate
Her heart so pure – and love so deep
Her sorrow for me – rocky and steep

       The mother I used to be
       locked in jail, not hers to see

Letters come – with pencil lead
Maybe she'll read them – before going to bed
Maybe she'll cry – or rip it in two
and mourn the seven years of sobriety which I blew
Maybe she'll give up on me here and now
or again trust me – if she can learn how

       Of all the things
       I regret, I despise,
       Is the way that addiction
       came back – telling lies.

## Chords

*Cole Crandell*

It's through these strings my soul can vent
My fingers bleed my heart's content.
And so to you it's just a chord
But my heart and soul are aboard.

## Pictures

*Cole Crandell*

A glimpse of life
A quick click of shutter
Leaves memories of time spent with each other.
I'm thankful for pictures
Most every day,
For they remind me why
It hurts to be away

## A True Friend

*Misty Lakin*

a true friend
is someone you know
and they know you...

a true friend
is someone who
can sense your fears
and wipe your tears...

a true friend
is someone who
will go out of their way for you
just to say "I'm only a phone call away..."

a true friend
is someone who
will always speak what's on their mind
but hold that place for you in their heart
but you gotta hold up your bargain and do your part.

That's what a true friend is – someone you love and trust
and can count on in every way and every day.

## When I was Small

*Dennis Brown*

When I was small in the spring, summer, fall and winter we had different camps. I remember most of all the spring and fall.

In the spring we would go to Maple Sugar Camp or Sugar Bush Camp. There were a few teepees set up to sleep in. It was all traditional. We would cook on the campfire, eat a lot of traditional food and berries after we tapped the trees. We used coffee cans to catch the sap we collected to boil down to make syrup, candy and sugar. There was a lot of time to play after we did what had to be done. At night we would sit around the camp fire and listen to the elders tell stories. There were always stories to hear and most were to learn from. There were also funny ones, old ones, family ones, and tribal ones. Sugar bush was fun.

In the fall we had Wild Rice Camp. I only went a few times but it was some of the most fun I've ever had. When I was young, we packed up the boats weeks before and my family would be making rice knockers and poles from fresh cedar wood to go out on the lake. We had food tents and all the camping equipment. It was all traditional stuff. At daybreak my family would head out on the lake and go ricing. Our camp was same as Sugar Bush except instead of a big barrel to boil down the sap there was a barrel to keep the rice. We kids would make rice shakers out of birch bark and birch baskets and dream catchers. We were taught how to fan the rice so it is ready for curing. Most rice we sold raw. Some we kept for the winter.

In the spring when there was still some snow on the ground, no leaves on the trees, there was the smell of spring after a long winter. In the fall the leaves are beautifully colored, the air is crisp, the water is still warm and we swam every day. It is fun to be a traditional Indian.

## The Eraser

*Julie Bolton*

An eraser is so hard to find in jail.
Who knew?

And then I found it was simply solved
by using my shoe!

## When Are You Coming Home

*Aaron Patterson*

A father makes a mistake.
Families suffer,
A small boy, a son, his son,
He calls, no answer.
Dad, where are you?
No answer.
Dad calls.
Dad, where are you?
I need you and want you.
When are you coming home?
Soon. How soon?
Why can't I come see you?
When are you coming home?
I miss you, I want you.
I need you, Dad.
When are you coming home?

## SIDS

*Frank Pavlacky*

Since your very first breath
From your very first smile
And your very first laugh,
I still don't know why they can't
Explain this death.
I cried and cried
Not knowing how or why.
People say it will get better and
God knows best,
But my heart still hurts day and night
Because I still don't understand
This sudden infant death.

## Color Blind

*Anthoni McMorris-Rice*

For the one who is blind, color is of no importance,
Is of no significance,
For he cannot appreciate the joyful yellows,
Cool blues, vibrant reds, delicate purples,
Or even the dull grays, mournful blacks
And lifeless whites.

For the one who can see, color is depreciated,
Is of little significance,
For he takes for granted his sight,
As if it were supposed to have been given to him,
As if it were a mandatory gift.

Perhaps one should switch fates with the other,
See what, at first, could not have been sought,
Appreciate what has been depreciated,
Understand the significance in what was believed
        to be insignificant.

Now he who once took for granted his sight
Has become filled with sorrow.
He mourns the loss of his vision.
His eyes have become useless,
Now as lifeless as the whites the blind man
At first could not see.

## Presents

*Dale Payne III*

In this room I cry
As the hardest parts of me die.
Crumbled away is an angry shell;
I left all the pain in my cell.
Lights shine in the distance
Feeling so alone on this Christmas.

Criminals, outcasts of society
Those people stand beside me.
Tendencies that make us evil,
My actions even to me unbelievable.

What do we all want for Christmas?
To hear our loved ones say they miss us.

## Lyrics

*Chris Finn Jr.*

In my mind's eye I despise who I've been;
In the mirror I see a foe and a friend
Locked in this concrete room.
It's like a concrete womb,
A chance to be reborn.
Too many times I've been forewarned
Where I was going
And how I'd be my own undoing
By letting my anger explode
Leaving me exposed.
So I pray to the Lord,
My spiritual sword,
Though I walk through the valley of the shadow of death
I shall fear no evil.
Through my lyrics
Let my spirit fly like an eagle

**Dear Meth,**

I am writing you this letter to say one final farewell.
You were always there for me in my time of need.
When I needed a friend, you seemed to always be around.
You have made me laugh; you have made me cry.
When I was feeling down, you lifted me high.
However, I will no longer lie,
You've cost me too much:
My home, my family, my pride, my soul.
You never really made me feel whole.
I lost my freedom.
But I'll tell you the truth: I've been having an affair
       this whole time I've been locked away.
I've found a new friend, a new love, an everlasting friend.
It loves me, it cares about me, it has gifted me
With the luxuries that, for so long, you seemed to rob me of.
Loyalty, honesty, integrity!
The name of the love that's replaced you is Sobriety.
It's here on my terms, by my choice.
It doesn't rob me of anything,
But instead, allows me to grow spiritually and honestly.
It's guiding me down a path to a life of happiness that
I've longed for and desired for some time now.
Please try to understand,
As much as you once meant to me,
I can no longer afford to invest in our dysfunctional relationship.
My new love has cost me nothing, nor will it ever.
As selfish as it may sound,
I am taking my 77 days of sobriety
And bidding you one last farewell.
I am sorry things didn't work out for us.
Please know I'll always remember what an impact you had on my life
For the last couple years.
For the permanent scars you've caused,
You'll always be remembered,
Just not celebrated.

       Never truly yours,
       Annie

## Understand

*Derek Blakely*

Understand I am a man that makes mistakes
Just like you.
Understand my mistakes are no different from ones
You chose to do.
My faults are your faults
And you I understand.
We are no better than one another.
God created equal men
Lying, cheating and stealing.
Now we're telling war stories together
Because we didn't do it right.
Truth be told,
In crime there never was a right way

## From the Inside Out

*Derek Blakely*

I was testing the waters, dancing with crime,
Loving the drugs until I got lost in time.
Success is a struggle inside and out.
Physically I'm poor,
Mentally lost, but my mind's asking for more.
My dreams are a gift, so I dream to be free.
Hey you out there, are you dreaming 'bout me?
My children I love, only them I will cherish.
The love we share makes others fear us.
No matter the struggle, no matter the time,
No longer givin' up sweet children of mine.
I ask for forgiveness, inside I want peace,
But in my mind I'm a rebel stuck in the streets.
Poverty is real and it lives right next door;
I'm hurting my own by feeding it more.
Addiction and struggle are very real;
I danced with them both, these feelings I feel.
Today is a struggle, but I will succeed.
Tomorrow never ends till my soul and spirit is freed.
It's always a battle that never will end.
I'll see you again, and be good, my friend.

## Myself

*Patrick Aleman*

Opening up of a flower,
hope so high.
Letting the willow trees
Sway on by.

Hearts are so still
watching the day daisies bloom fulfill.
Wonderment, confusion, everlasting trust,
these are things that are just a must.

Leveling the playing field,
allowing acts to be,
the glass is half full,
I know you will see.

Loving the wonder, enjoying the game
I know others will see,
they are all the same.

In the end there is nothing,
only just to be

## Here I Go Again

*William Desjarlais*

Where did I go wrong? I just got out of this place. I wasn't even out that long! Tellin' my family, all my friends, "Okay no more going back," but it never ends! Here I am back in this hell, sittin' in my cell, makin' promises to myself! Now I'm no criminal, definitely no psycho, guess you can say I'm stuck in a vicious cycle. Nobody but bricks to keep me company, prayin' to God the judge doesn't throw the book at me! As I sit here wishin' to hear from a friend, all I can think to myself is, "Here I go again".

## Anger

*Dale Payne III*

An anger once burned inside me
One I pointed directly at society
Everything that was I destroyed
Shattered homes and broke dreams

What about your beautiful family?
Through gritted teeth I reply angrily
All gone

But
"Daddy," she says,
"I love you."

My heart beats a moment longer;
Thank God I'm a father.
The rage inside me subsided.
Though my family is divided,
Hopes and dreams are in my mind again

## Hard Time

*Joe Roberts*

Time is here to stay, but never does ours last,
Memories of loved ones slip slowly into the past.
Sun and moon will come, plus many, many more,
But never again will we walk together on that abandoned shore.
Not knowing how to ever allow you to fade away,
It keeps me always asking for one more endless day.
Everything to you was more fragile than priceless art,
You accomplished so much in so little time, mostly filling my heart.
I miss when time mattered only to the waking stars,
Now it just shows me that I'm unhealable, fading into my scars.
No matter how long I decide to deal with this futile climb,
I know that pain still hurts and will until the end of my time.

## Time

*Dillon Forrest*

What is time?
Time is anything.
Time is simply this.
Time is a creation within the minds that bend and twist.
What is time?
Time is powerful.
Time refuses to desist.
Time is a heavy hammer clenched within an iron fist.
What is time?
Time is memory.
Time is full of bliss.
Time is just a fragment of the moments that we missed.
What is time?
Time is everything.
Time is all there is.
Time is so important that we keep it wrapped around our wrists.
What is time?
Time is magical.
Time is just a wish.
Time is neither here nor there so how can time exist?
What is time?

## Problems

*Heather Holmberg*

I think of all my problems,
I think of all my pain,
I think of all my sorrows
Until I go insane.

I think of all the smiles I've worn
Which hide my sorrows underneath.
No one seems to notice
I go through so much grief.

Tears continue flowing
Out of my tired eyes.
Each time I try to tell you,
My words come out as lies.

These days I'm feeling distant,
Far away and weak,
When sunshine and happiness
is all I truly seek.

## Paint Chips

*Randberg*

Paint chips falling on my bed,
Teardrops falling from my head.
Yearning for my mom
Cellmate says Stay strong
This time of year I can't hear
My families' voices so near.
Missing my girl's voice
Knowing I made the wrong choice.
So here I sit
Doing a six-month bit
Watching paint chips fall.
Chips in the wall
Like dimples on the skin,
Knowing all along
I just can't win
Watching paint chips fall.

## There's a Toll on My Soul

*Hunter Vidnar*

There's a toll on my soul
My heart's a black hole.
I feel empty inside like
There's no more life to be lived.
I'm useless not being with my kid;
He needs a dad – no, he needs a father,
Someone who will be there
And help him ride a bike
Or fly a kite.
But I'm nowhere in sight.
That puts a toll on my soul.

My son is my sun;
He's my world, my light.
I have to still fight with all my might,
But there's no end in sight
To all my anguish and despair.
I just wish I could care for my child,
But my charges are not mild.
So it seems impossible to smile
While in Fox* with all these locks
And bland white cinder blocks.
There's no one to blame,
And it fills me with shame
And takes a toll on my soul.

*\* Fox is the name of one housing unit in Crow Wing County Jail*

## My Leaf

*Larry Bolton*

What is it like outside?
Oh! There was a small leaf on the floor outside my jail cell
Must have been stuck to the jailer's shoe
What a surprise to find a piece of nature
In this high-tech sanitary environment
A virtual oddity
How long will it be until I see another leaf in this place?
There was a fly once, another time a spider
Other inmates witnessed these events
Time for a nap and slowly one more day
On the way to see another leaf

## Again

*Larry Bolton*

The leaf is brown
It was found on the floor
Its next location was behind the phone in the bubble
It lasted about three weeks
Now this little leaf of ours
Is resting on the call intercom plate
In cell 115L Fox unit
At the time of this writing
It has been in this location for two weeks
Stay tuned for more adventures of the leaf

## Invisibility

*Anthoni McMorris-Rice*

One who sees doesn't always fully comprehend what is being sought.
Open eyes don't always see.
Sometimes you can see more when your eyes are shut.
Walking down a path which has no lighting,
Nothing illuminating the path, can most certainly be a difficult
journey, a dangerous adventure.
Walking down a road where darkness engulfs nature as flames do
a burning house.
Oh, how I would love to see my future.
Oh, how I have dreamed of a freedom
So pure, so righteous without any attachment,
without any returning services for my servitude.
No matter how much strain I cause upon my eyes,
No matter how strong the prescription,
or how clear my glasses are,
I will never be able to see my future if I continue to watch my past.
For my past is the path I speak of,
The path of darkness in which I wander about aimlessly with no
lighting; nothing illuminating the path.
For if I so choose to continue down the path, my soul will become
that of darkness
And my spirit will be submerged in the sea of blackness.

## Mmmm......

*Steve Whitney*

Pecan pie, Cool Whip
Fried chicken, extra crispy
Flaky buttered biscuits,
Corn on the cob with creamy cheese and hot sauce
Pulled pork sandwiches
Those little smokies with barbecue sauce that you pick up with a
toothpick,
Meat and cheese and crackers
Frisco burger
Curly fries
Mmmmmm
Coleslaw
Big salad with baby tomatoes, fresh spinach, eggs, bacon bits, sun-
flower seeds, cucumbers, black olives with ranch or blue cheese
on them.
Mmmmmm
And cottage cheese on the side
Fried fish with tartar sauce.
Etc., etc.

## The Tears I've Cried

*Jesse Walbeck*

The tears I've cried, for the time I've lost.
The tears I've cried, for the things I've lost.
The tears I've cried, for the things I've done.
The tears I've cried, for what's to come.
The tears I've cried, for the pain I've caused.
The tears I've cried, for the people I've lost.
The tears I've cried, for the way I've been treated,
The tears I've cried, for the dreams I've lost.
The tears I've cried, for the people in here.
The tears I've cried, 'cause it seems no one can hear.
The tears I've cried, for the unanswered letters.
The tears I've cried, for the things in my past.
The tears I've cried, for the sacrifices I've made.
The tears I've cried, for the Lord these days.
The tears are wiped away by the Lord Jesus Christ.
Amen

## My Open Heart

*Tyson D. Neddo*

I was skeptical on what I should display,
Worrying about pushing you away.
Your encouragement makes it easy for me to speak,
So that now I don't feel so weak.

I'm never alone, but sometimes lonely
Because real people are hard to find.
Being crowded by these phonies
Makes me second-guess my peace of mind.

Steady searching for you,
But my words are never spoken.
My closed mouth won't be heard, so therefore,
My open heart will never be broken.
Our day will come when we, as lovers,
Will learn more about each other,
Remaining friends, although naïve
To what is yet to be discovered.
For a strong bond to be created,
It may seem forever to achieve,
But capable of being unbreakable
Is not hard for me to believe.

We always want the trust
Because we both have been mistrusted,
Stepping out on empty promises,
Set our hearts up only to be busted.
Neither of us should be judged
On what has happened in our past.
We all have made mistakes
From making decisions way too fast . . .

How much would it be worth
If we could turn righteous overnight?
Being patient makes it priceless,
So let's take our time and do this right.

Many people make an issue out of sex,
Which is the least of my concern.
I believe anyone can misuse the body,
But your heart I would rather earn . . .

I know you were true from the start,
So for you I offer my open heart.

## Don't Look Back

*Anna Sebasky*

I may be a broken person
fragmented and distorted.
Because I could not bear my past,
to drugs I finally resorted.

I can't claim that I believed
that I could live like this forever,
but I didn't know how bad it could be,
or I wouldn't have done it ever.

An addiction is like a machine
and the drug is its fuel.
You think you're in control
but you're not and the world's cruel.

You crave the feeling that it gives;
You chase after it day by day;
You say you're going to quit,
but that's too easy to say.

Why would anyone expect you to stop
when it feels all too good?
They just don't understand it.
If only there was a way they could.

If they knew how it feels,
that crazy, euphoric rush,
They'd never ask you to quit.
They knew it'd be asking too much.

So what if it's poison?
Even killing you, too.
But you've lost control now
without it you don't know what you'd do.

Everyone can see it now.
The addiction has changed you.
So now that you admit that
where's the person they once knew?

It's time to rise up
out of the depth of your habit,
and if someone reaches out to help,
strain to reach their hand and grab it.

It's not going to be easy
to get your life on track,
but you can win the war
if you move forward and don't look back.

## My If Only

*Trillium*

My love; my if only
The crow has captured me
          no longer shall I be free
Oh how my heart does flood
          filled with tears of blood
Such passions drown in pain
          red tears fall in vain
Forsaken we must be
          to a life in agony
I wish that I could breathe
          air fresh from the trees
To feel the sun on my skin
          to kiss my lover again
Why can't we be free
          to laugh
                    to love
                              to live joyously
A life in the light
          with no need to fight
Out of this cage
          of Crow Wing County Rage

## Tears Upon My Face

*Carla Gale*

Here I am once again
sitting inside this cell.
I tried and tried to maintain balance
but once again I fell.

Oh my dear child of mine
why is it you can't see.
It is 'YOU' who keeps steering yourself
from the sight of me!

But, my Lord I'm tired and weak
I feel I have no more fight.
I keep choosing a path so wrong
no matter how much I want it right!

Oh my dear child, why can't you see,
There's a lesson I'm trying to teach,
It's you who has to choose your own path
no matter how hard I preach!

But my Lord how many times
to this place must I return,
Before I finally understand
the lesson I am to learn?

My dear Lord I need your guidance
when it's time to leave this place,
I'm on my knees to you my Lord,
with tears upon my face.

## OMG! I DON'T BELONG HERE!!!

*Caroline Jochum*

What happens to a person who is put in jail
For a crime she did not commit?
She gets a cell 8 x 10
She gets a bed 2 x 6
She gets her meals 1 x 3
She gets a box 1 x 1

No one believes she didn't do the crime
'Cause they see she has been committed...
She gets a blue shirt
She gets blue pants
She gets a brown bra
She gets brown underpants

She sits alone in a great big room wanting to cry,
but she dare not and can't.
She gets an account
She gets a phone card
She gets some supplies
She gets some meds

One brick, two bricks, three bricks, four
When can I see the front door?

*This poem illustrated on next page*

**Bricks** *Caroline Jochum*

**Flying Bird** *Shane Addison*

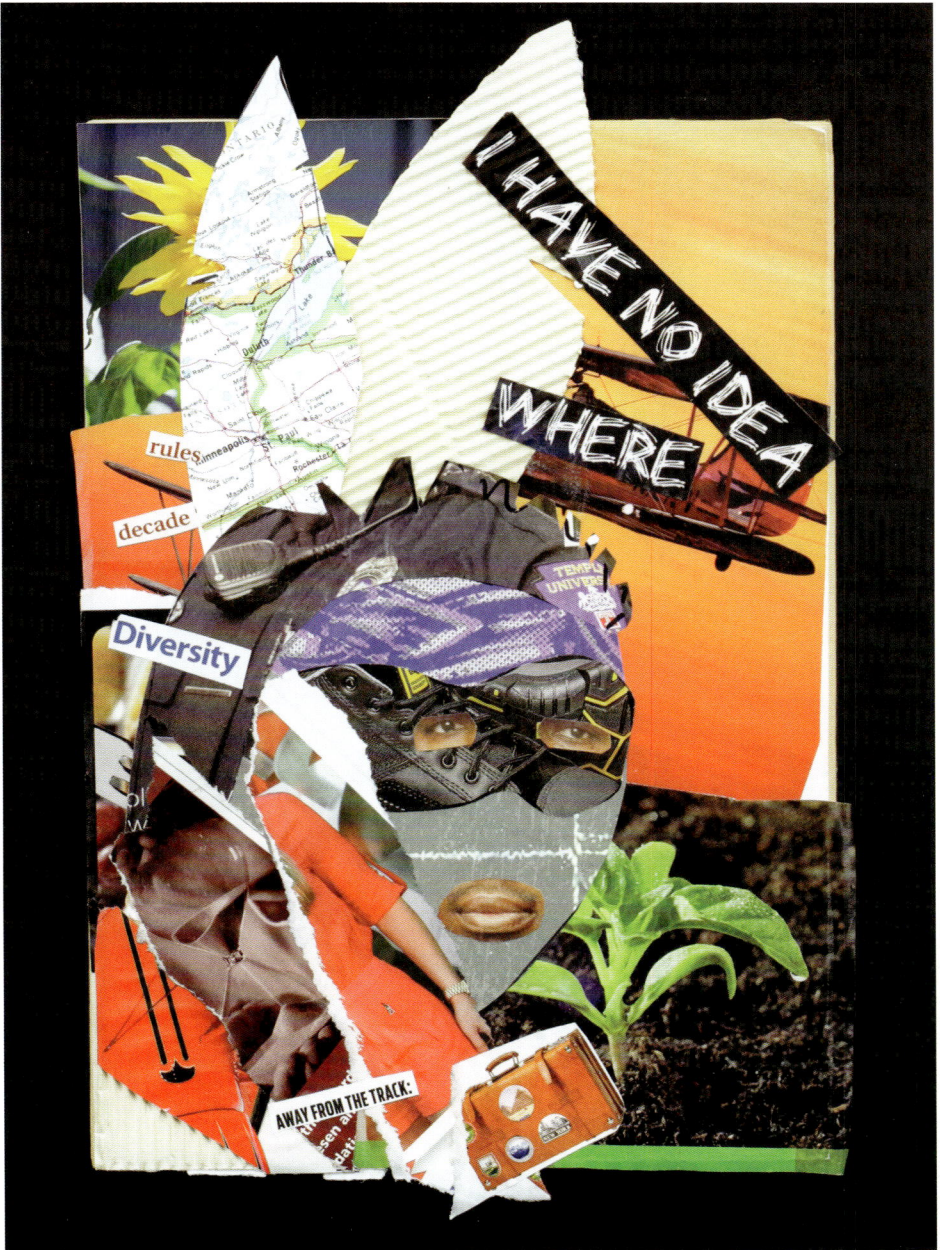

**Stuff We Take for Granted**  *Patrick Aleman*

**Blue Butterfly** *Patrick Aleman*

**Moon Sprite** *Patrick Aleman*

**Love** *Josephine Andrews*

**Bladesmith** *Larry Bolton*

**Untitled** *Dane Brogle*

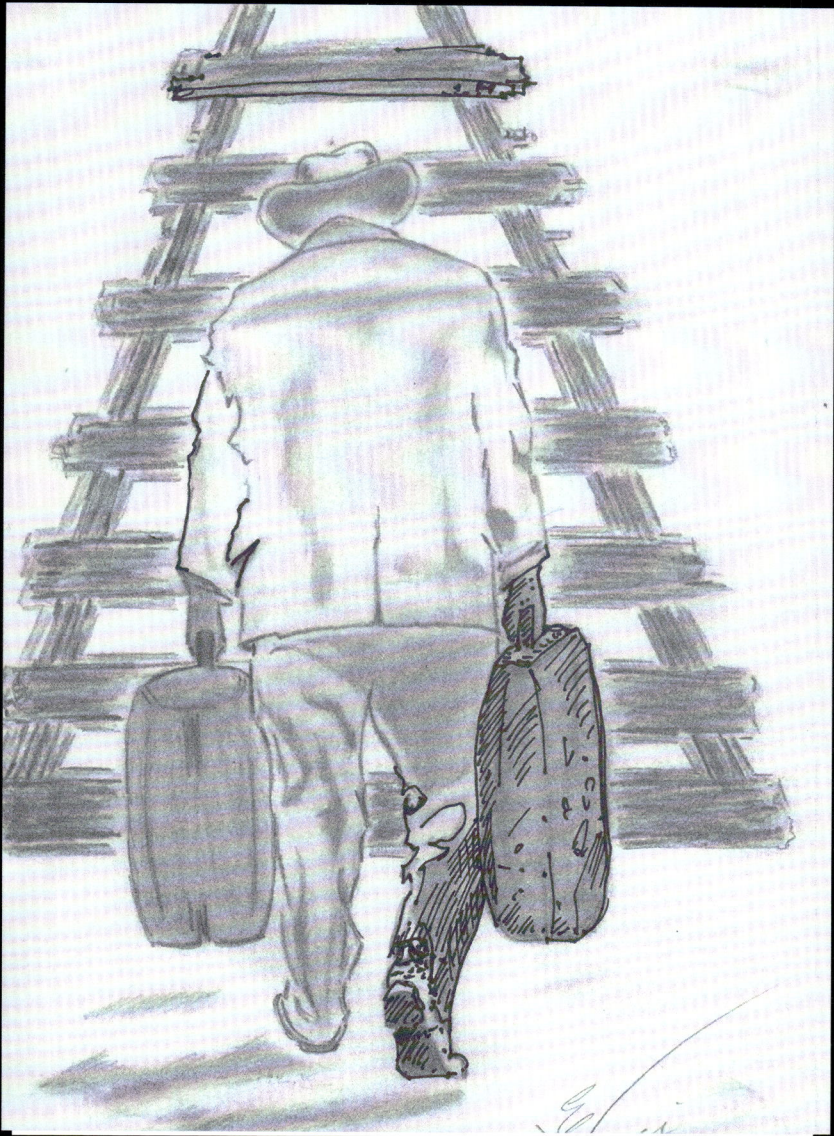

**My Journey** *Name Withheld*

**Native** *Dennis Brown*

**I Love My Sons** *Jaz Carillo*

**Missing You** *Kenny Cloud*

**Goodyear** *Ray Ellis*

**Wolf** *Charles Fairbanks*

**Untitled** *Charles Fairbanks*

**We Shall Remain - Happy People** *Evan Fasthorse*

**Nascar** *Evan Fasthorse*

**Untitled** *Carla Gale*

**Boat** *Dan Haggenmiller*

**Untitled**  *Kaylee Hathaway*

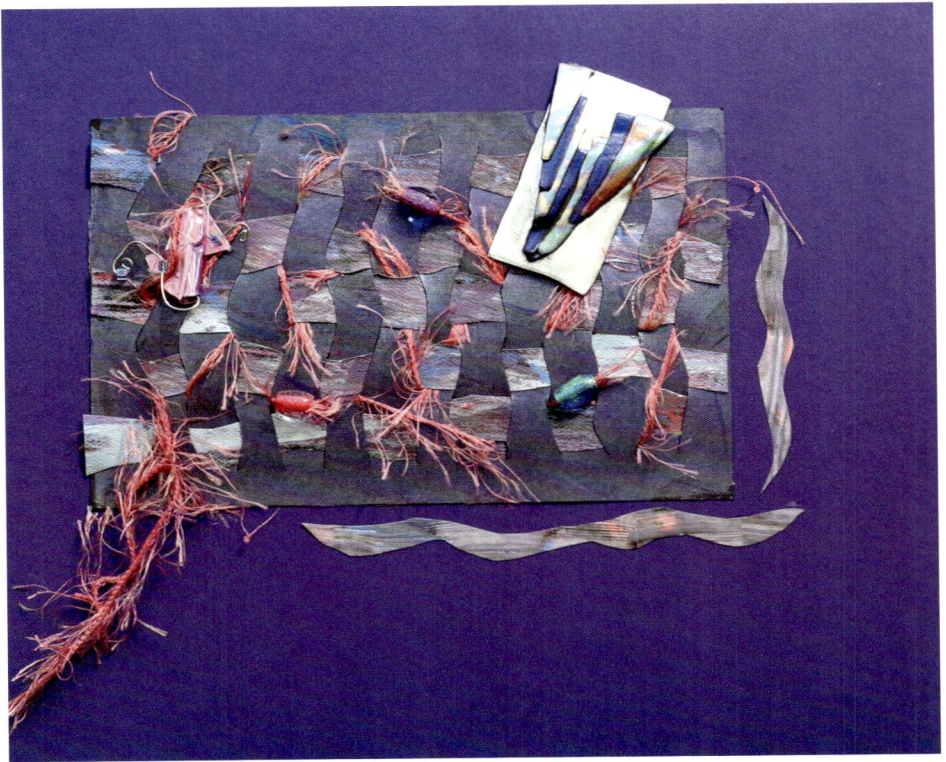

**Untitled** *Danielle Isham*

**Travel** *Caroline Jochum*

**Renew**  *Sabrina Johnson*

**Untitled** *Amber Johnson*

**Wisdom** *Amber Johnson*

**Jingle Dress Dancer** *Amber Johnson*

**Pin-Up Beauty** *Amber Johnson*

**Untitled**  *Devin Jothanh*

**Native Then & Now**  *Kingbird*

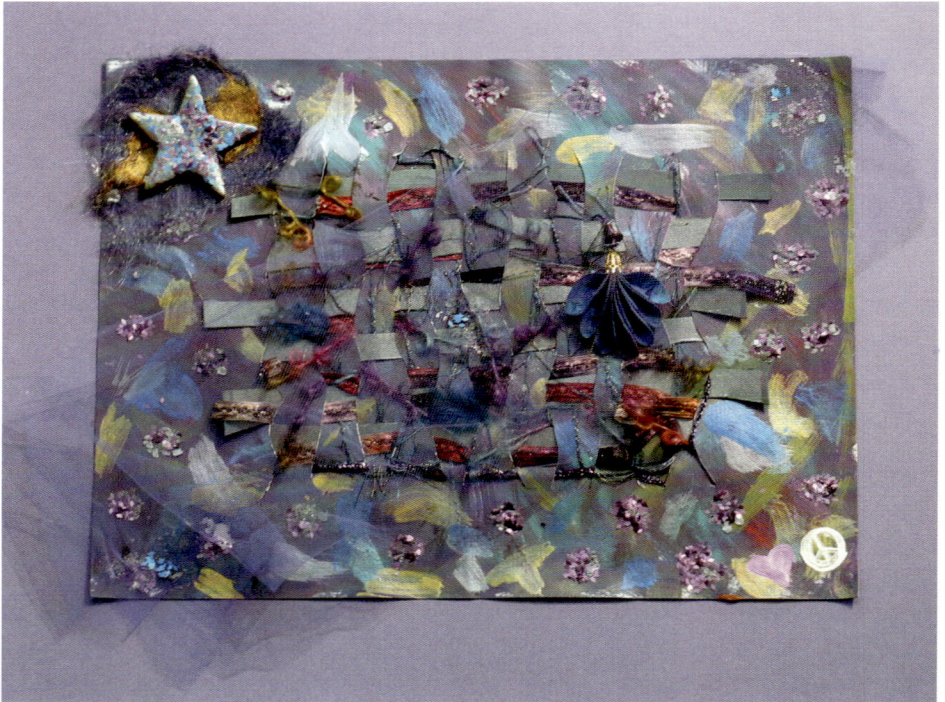

**Untitled**  *Tori Litteral*

**Untitled** *Samuel Lyons*

We the Willing  *Doug Melby*

**Missing You** *Doug Melby*

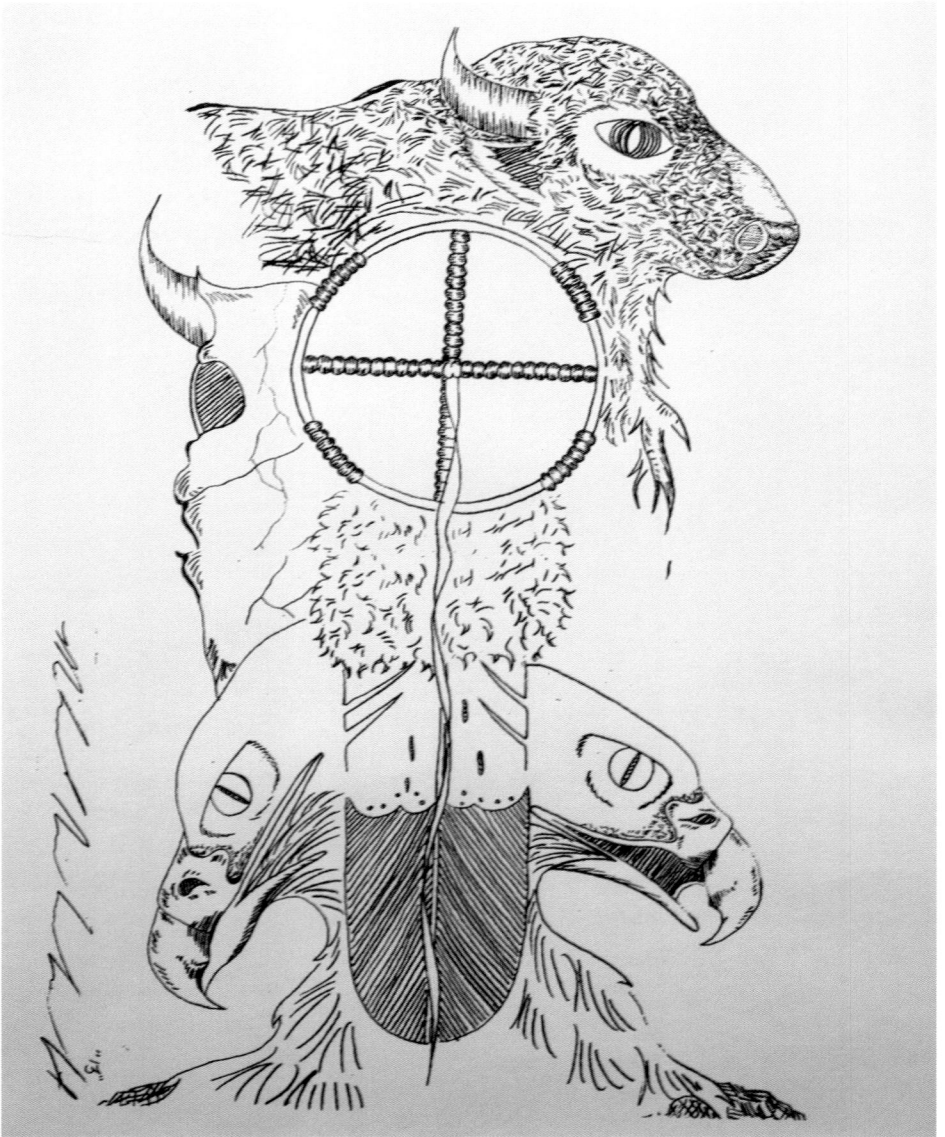

**Untitled** *Name Withheld*

**Untitled** *Name Withheld*

How can I forget you when
your always on my mind!
How can I not want you when
your all I want inside!
How can I let you go when
I cant see us apart?
How can I not Love you when
you control my HEART!

**How Can I Forget You** *Tyson Neddo*

**Fearless**  *Celeste Nelson-Raba*

**Untitled** *Colleen Patrick*

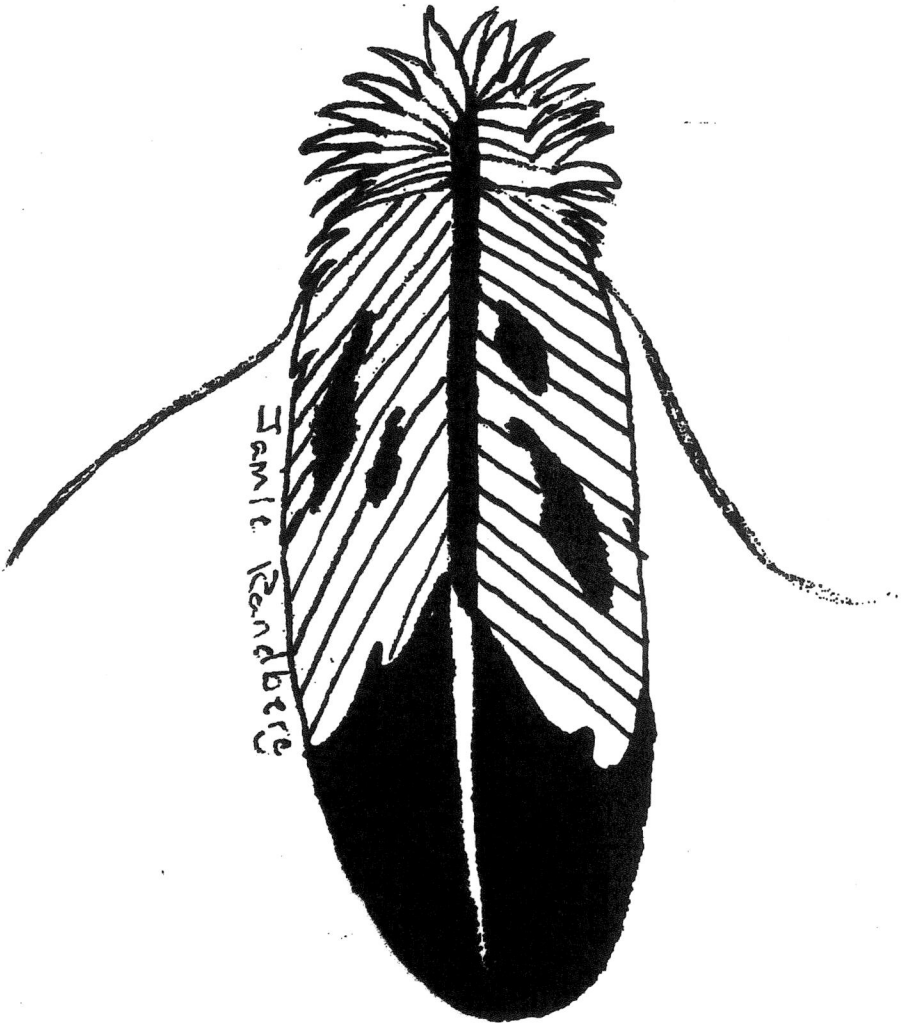

**Untitled** *Randberg*

**Best in Show** *Jack Smith*

**Eagle** *Jack Smith*

**Untitled** *Mel Smith*

**Untitled** *Mel Smith*

**Hope**  *Hope Strey*

**Lost Cause** *John Treece*

**Untitled** Yang

**Around the Metro** *Yang*

**Untitled** *Yang*

**Hang Glider** *Name Withheld*

**I'm Not Perfect** *Kerri Zelinski*

**Lady in Blue** *Kerri Zelinske*

Moments of Imagination *Nat*

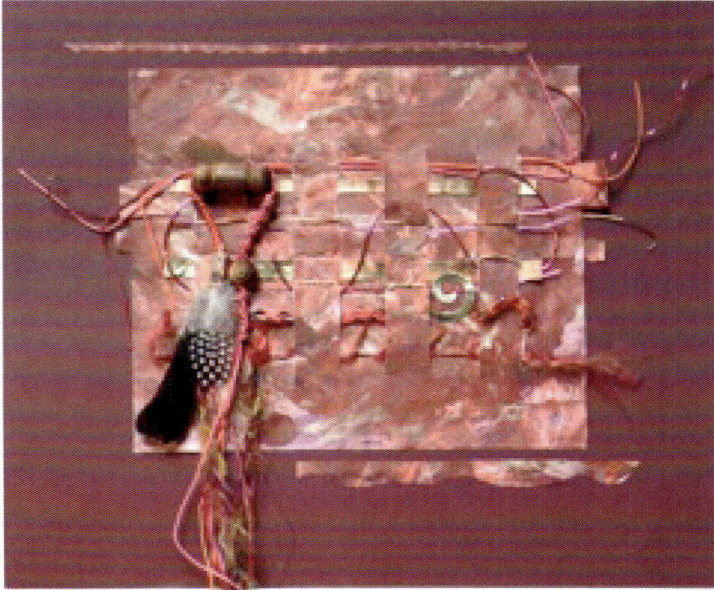

Coolness *Nat*

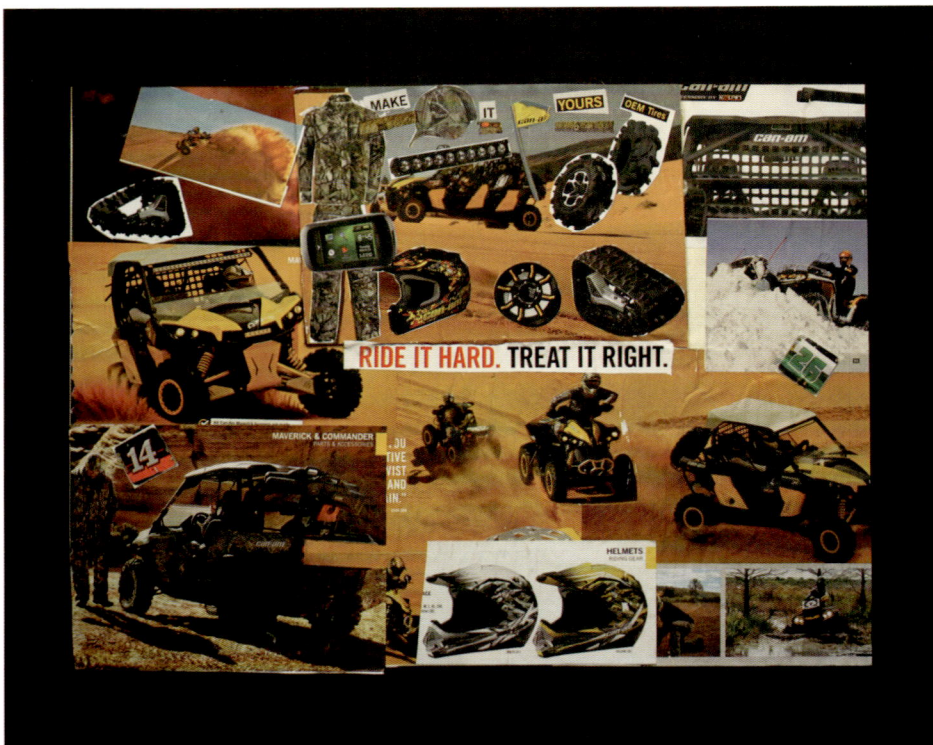

**Ride it Hard** *Eric*

At the end of the day, we must go forward with hope
and not backward by fear and division.
~ *Jesse Jackson*

# COMPANION LIST

In an effort to connect inmates to the wider artistic community, the Crossing Arts Alliance (TCAA) offered an opportunity for literary and visual artists outside the jail to select work made by the incarcerated and create companion pieces to complement and enhance the originals. The response, with more than fifty works selected, exceeded expectations. Beyond the Bricks, the culmination of the Jail Arts Project, is an exhibit of original and companion pieces open to the public for a limited time at Franklin Arts Center in Brainerd, MN. For further information see the TCAA web site: www.crossingarts.org.

Although their work does not appear in this publication, community contributors to this project are greatly appreciated. TCAA extends recognition to the following:

Mary Aalgaard
Bev Abear
Lily Atwel
Corey Beach
Carol Bombardier
Janice Bradshaw
Kate Carlson
Charmaine Donovan
Roberta Doucette
Carol Eliseuson
John Erickson
Bonnie Fercho
Phyllis Frankum
Audrae Gruber
Haddie Hadachek
Elsie Husom
Charlie Johnson
Lowell Johnson
Lisa Jordan
Deanne Joy
Lonnie Knutson
Kathy Krueger

Julie Jo Larson
Colleen LeBlanc
Jan Lendobeja
Evelyn Matthies
Barbara Morgan
Brenda Myers
Martin Nelson
Lauren Nickisch
Mike Paulus
Brenda Pfeffer
Catherine Rausch
Greg Rosenberg
Diane Runberg
Amy Sharpe
Candace Simar
Rhonda Smith
Sue Smith-Grier
Krista Soukup
Doris Stengel
Jane Stevens
Maria Thompson-Seep
Pam Warren

At the end of the day, we must go forward with hope
and not backward by fear and division.

~ *Jesse Jackson*

# COMPANION LIST

In an effort to connect inmates to the wider artistic community, the Crossing Arts Alliance (TCAA) offered an opportunity for literary and visual artists outside the jail to select work made by the incarcerated and create companion pieces to complement and enhance the originals. The response, with more than fifty works selected, exceeded expectations. Beyond the Bricks, the culmination of the Jail Arts Project, is an exhibit of original and companion pieces open to the public for a limited time at Franklin Arts Center in Brainerd, MN. For further information see the TCAA web site: www.crossingarts.org.

Although their work does not appear in this publication, community contributors to this project are greatly appreciated. TCAA extends recognition to the following:

| | |
|---|---|
| Mary Aalgaard | Julie Jo Larson |
| Bev Abear | Colleen LeBlanc |
| Lily Atwel | Jan Lendobeja |
| Corey Beach | Evelyn Matthies |
| Carol Bombardier | Barbara Morgan |
| Janice Bradshaw | Brenda Myers |
| Kate Carlson | Martin Nelson |
| Charmaine Donovan | Lauren Nickisch |
| Roberta Doucette | Mike Paulus |
| Carol Eliseuson | Brenda Pfeffer |
| John Erickson | Catherine Rausch |
| Bonnie Fercho | Greg Rosenberg |
| Phyllis Frankum | Diane Runberg |
| Audrae Gruber | Amy Sharpe |
| Haddie Hadachek | Candace Simar |
| Elsie Husom | Rhonda Smith |
| Charlie Johnson | Sue Smith-Grier |
| Lowell Johnson | Krista Soukup |
| Lisa Jordan | Doris Stengel |
| Deanne Joy | Jane Stevens |
| Lonnie Knutson | Maria Thompson-Seep |
| Kathy Krueger | Pam Warren |